You are what Matters

My life with You

Written by Alvaro A. Cardoza

Illustrations by Patricia V Mendez

 ISBN: 9798709837928

DEDICATION

In my heart, I belong to all of you. I wait for our time to be together under the sunshine. More words to describe how I will always feel about you. I love you.

CONTENTS

ACKNOWLEDGMENTS

Patricia is a young artist and did an incredible job with the cover of this book and the pictures for all of these poems. All profits made from this book will go to her

Patricia's ACKNOLEDGEMENTS

I would like to start off by thanking my mom for finding this opportunity. I appreciate how my mom and dad sees my potential in my art. I would like to thank Mr. Alvaro for letting me illustrate this book. I thank my family for looking at each illustration and motivating me that I can do this. I would like to thank my 2 closest friends as well for knowing and encouraging me that I can do this. I never thought in a million years I would have illustrated a book. This is an amazing opportunity, and I am beyond grateful.

When I kiss you and I press my lips against yours. As your mouth opens slowly to receive my tongue into yours. The pleasures begin to rise to heights above heights.

I begin getting lost and without hesitation, I continue kissing you. I drown into your passion with mine. My air my reasons my wants being engulfed by your sweet taste.

There is no plain, no existing source of living that would nurture anywhere close to the creation sensation you drive from the outside of me to the inside of my living soul.

Awakening me into a reality of life that I can call mine. You are mine. The truest statement will be true and real. You are the defining moment of incredible.

Anyone can say they wish they could touch the stars just to know what it would be like. I have touched eternity with you.

Bliss haven with you

The song of your soul
sings to my heart.

My heart begins to
flow with incredible
energy.

The never-ending energy
of what we hold
is a fortune amassed
all limits that no
one knows.

What you must know
is what I already
think.

That you and I will
always be.

You, I

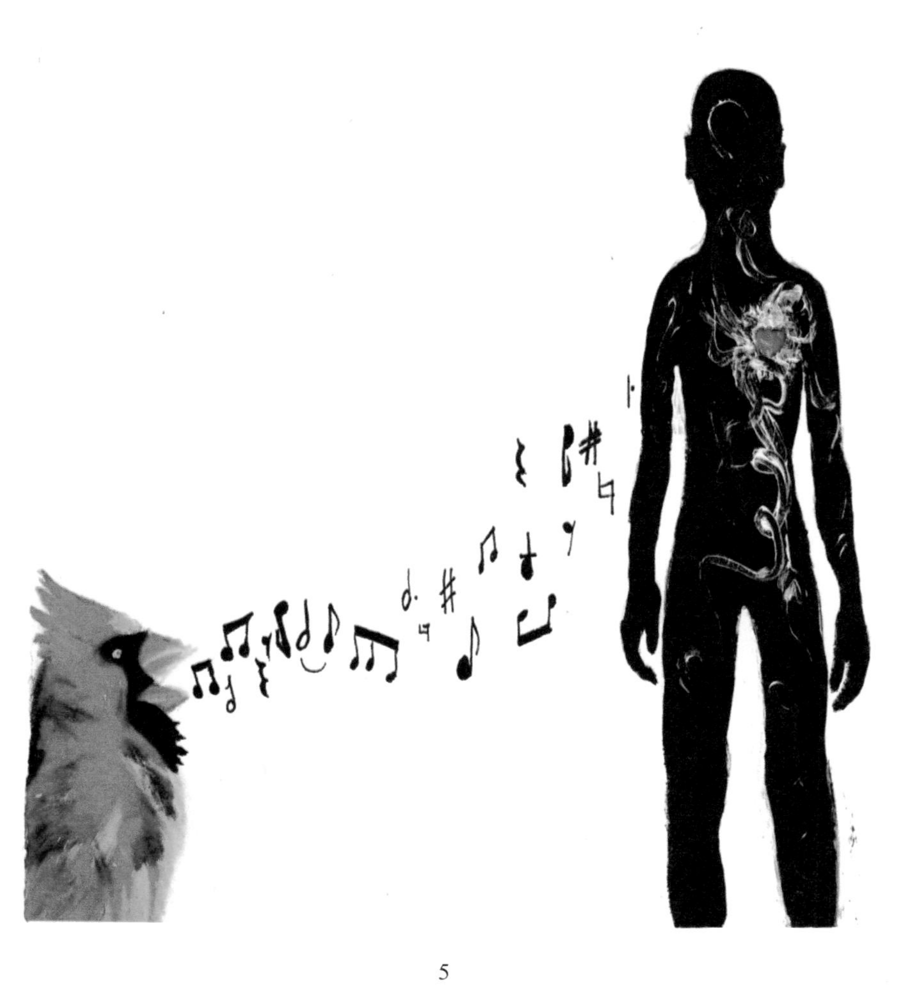

Fell in love, rush of life full of excite.

Strong night inside my soul back alive.

Met you, now I stay

I find both the vast universe idyllic meaning and the notion of the world's beauty up swirled into what I can only think God would define as beautiful when I look into those eyes of yours.

I find myself in truest space of faithful peace full of indulging life held with no lies when I am raptured by your body that speaks to only me. And by design sings to my soul.

I find eternity and a day and another day to be the only amount of significant time that I want, desire, and need to spend it with you. Any less would never quench the ever need of my life side by side with you.

I find never to question the why you. The parallel of time met the crease of love, the line of fate, and the corner of you and I at the same place to be what was always to become to be.

I find myself gaze stranded where only you and I exist. I know I was not there at the beginning. I will be there the rest of the way.

Gaze stranded

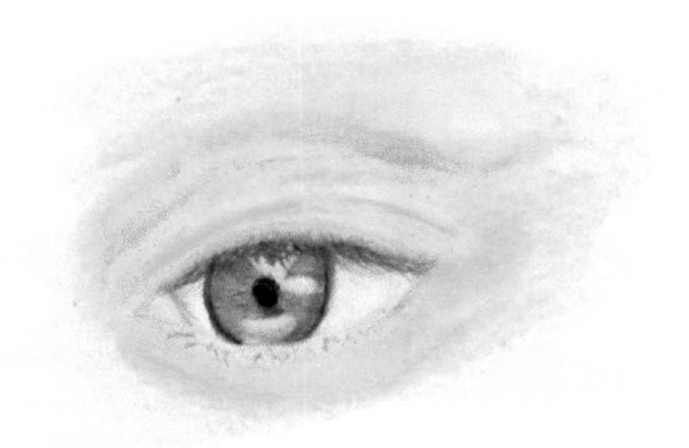

There are no melodies that I can put into words to sing you a song about how much you mean to me.

There are no totality of words I could place together to let you know how much I love you.

There are no simple array of stars that could be forced destined to show you just how bright you make my soul.

I just want you, need you to know that I love you.

No song I can write

The bounties of perfect shaped diamonds are just abled speckled coal that only under pressure broke through to create beauty.

I know not any of a story as to how you came to be the beautiful defined by limited wording that you are today.

Your past, your present, you are undeniably like a cluster of galaxies that came to together. Slammed and imploded to create once in a lifetime creation.

You unique in life, in dreams, in all streams of reality. I know the fortunate gift I received when I get another chance to get a moment of time spent with you.

One You

A devil finds himself when he commits himself to adore that which he can not have.

He notices how through such filling he conquers that which he can not have. And as he treasures that which is not his, she becomes his.

They become one.

The music of peace is not peace but absolution. His demon feeding on new fruit and in it his horns of fallen fall off.

New surrounds him he himself is renewed. He himself now feels when so long there was nothing no rhythm no tone.

He bleeds out his pores a light. If love could be fully manifested this would be it. He glows as all of him combust and regrows into something he never had been.

All this change grew because of what should have not been his. But she made him hers too and she too became alive.

For she was a single fruit of passion left there slowly fading into rot. A rot that would have stayed until end of days.

But she was saved and he was saved. And now as two, they live life whole and true.

A life of two

My heart is the stone that dropped and fell deep into the ocean's floor that is your soul.

Never to be removed.
Never to bask in sunlight for the warmth of your soul heats up my heart with love as your body heats up my body with life pleasures.

My heart is the stone for which you can rely on.

Never to drown for I will make sure you will always be able to stand above.
Never to need a filter, you are the purest of all.

My heart is the stone to guard you from all who would try to break you.

Never to turn on you.
Never to break under any pressure.

My heart is the stone that became a diamond when you hold it in your hand.

Never to be let go by you for this heart is yours to keep and be kept.
Never will my heart betray you for all me is for you.

My ocean, I, your stone

When you look directly into my eyes it is as if my heart is aligned with all stars all planets all existing suns upon suns letting in a shine that engulfs all streams of light.

Your heart holds my soul deep inside. You are the center of my world. The gravity that pulls me to you. The root that planted inside my heart and blossomed your soul intermixed with mine.

Every day I am given is a day of creation. A new level of love that continues growing and expanding. There is no limits to what my life, my love, my all will give you. You continue giving me all of you.

Touch me, hold me, kiss me, love me. I will do the same to you. I have envelope a memory of every part of you. I can close my eyes and hear every single time you have told me that you love me. I can feel your smile when I hear you speak.

I will carry you with me. Hand to hand, love with love, cherishing you never alone. I will keep you for I am yours kept already. Fate? Soulmates? Meant to be? Everything in between? It is all of the above. Always.

The center of the world

Here are words that you need to read and hear over and over again...

Why are you amazing to me?

You are not a once in a lifetime.
You are not just a person in one's life.
You are not just incredible for the qualities that make you.

You are a one time. For no one ever will be anywhere to match the beauty of yours in every way.

You are not just a person but a wonderment of creation. A woman that sparks bigger than even the biggest star in existence.

You are not just incredible. You are not described words you are above any written, spoken, defined words. You are infinity made into a soul of the woman I don't just want to be with but want and need to be with.

You, my desire

The meeting we had planned did not have a chance today.

And that's okay for life has real unplanned delays. And things that happen that will not cooperate.

The hardest of times of being apart will only bring us closer and make our love more beautiful than a work of art.

Our love stronger than any potion. Our love going further than any length of motion.

I love you forever and even more. It is you and you alone who I will always adore.

Day 10

All I want is to let you know that I will never let you go.

All I want is to show you, how stars glaze above watching you glow.

Your love keeps me held in such a treasure trove. One that extends every day our love shows.

We were at a point where our last point in our mind was that there would be new sunshine.

And then when our passion intersected, and you left not knowing what would come next.

That point I felt my heartbeat and I had fallen so deep. I fell in love with you.

All I want is to be yours true.

All I want

I fell in love with you.

It happened so quick that I was awestruck at how my heart went dead to inflate.

The usual torments that I would use to keep my heart at bay faded like the end of a bad storm.

The sadness that would grow towards the night before I would fall asleep stopped being there.

You changed my life. You made me realize my sense of worth, my sense of life, my sense of happiness.

You made me want to be better. You made me want to improve my life.

I fell in love with you.

In every way that is true. And the journey I walk now every step moving forward and growing I want you there with me.

I want to be there with you. I want to be in those very moments you need to be held but also those moments I can surprise you and hold you just because I love you.

I fell in love with you.

YOU

In many ways and in many words and in too little of time there are constant structure sentences I want to tell you.

And they all lead to three words with such deep meaning.

I love you.

Every remainder light is the day's end that begins the night's cycle are just a globe filling of a passionate love inside my heart that just strike with more life more strength that will always be attached to your soul.

I will not disappoint, and I will never dishonor everything that holds true inside of you. For all of it are all I cherish and want to grow with you.

No end to the endless journey of ours. A wake-up good morning a mid-afternoon I miss you. A nighttime goodnight and all of it attached to loving you in more steadfast trueness that would blind anyone that would attempt to break it.

Everlasting and forevermore. I will journey with you to whatever life paths bring us. And if there is a fork in our journey you better believe whatever steps you take forward to will be where I go to.

Significant to me

The mere thought of thinking about you makes me smile.

You are wind blowing on a clear day even when you are not there, I know you are.

You are beautiful in every way I will always attempt to try to describe.

You are wonderful in every way you are designed.

You are words of truth.

I just want you to know that I do care and will always choose you.

You mine

8004

Inhale and when exhaling the life, you feel coursing inside of you is the symbol of knowing you live and love true.

The life and want desire of you is stronger than any magnitude a magnet could hope for.

A strike of thunder blazingly fast lightning abyss brightness that share all tell all. My words will do the same. I am with her. I love her. She is the one for me. I will always be with her if she will have me.

No deceit existing in all glows of me. A sanctuary of your soul that can pass in and throughout all of it knowing all paths lead to you.

A scribbling writing to tell you the one constant connection that we can touch. You lean against me and me into you. Breathe me and kiss me and I will to you.

And in a chaotic mess of this world whether undecided or even the planetary screams it achieves do not zone out the rise brim explosions of the infinite fires of you are mine to love.

All this all more all said all implored are ways and more ways and more said that is said on how it is to love you. Mostly though, it is to be above any height and further than any line. Always true always will love you.

What it means to love you

No distance exists to fill in the length space of the love we have for each other.

No time frame occurs in the wheel of it that will ever exhibit how long forever is for each other.

No space darkens the light that flows from our lips when we kiss to our bodies when we touch and love.

No words whispered or out loud will say it enough. I love you.

Loving you eternally

Like a lotus flower bloomed in such tender yet forgloried beauty.

A strength in her to not be laid any hand on except to that whom she allows.

The stories I am sure she could tell, the luck any would have to be able to listen to them.

Time absolute could feel endless at the sanctity of knowing someone who flourishes amazing.

There is only one of her. And none like her.

Attempting to define an incredible woman like her I know I fail as only words can only do so much.

Beautiful, strong, amazing, wonderful. Basic words but such words that can say the striking resemblance of who she is and how she captivates so many.

She is herself. She is one I could only hope to know one day.

She, the lotus flower

Embracing you and watching you as you lay there in my arms with your eyes closed, I smile, knowing full well how fortunate of a man I am to lay next to a woman whose beauty not only strikes inside all of her soul but outreaches to every curve of her incredible addicting body.

I live, I wake, I know.

You are the every bit of a cycle of rarity that repeat will never be defined into any mold to be known again. I reach higher heights of love in every spent moment with you.

I love, I grow, I live.

In every life that we are given, there is purpose-made. My heart lives full within your ever-loving soul. I linked to you and you held with me. There is nothing more incredible than the opportunity to be the always in hearing your laughter. In making you smile. In being the man who will love you and make love to you always.

My wonder my all

Our distance may be physical but compares none to the glow in my heart when I wake.

Your scent exists ongoing even as it fades awaiting rejuvenate, I smile knowing you were there.

When we talk even eyes closed, I hear that beautiful smile light up.

I know only what I know. What I know is that through whatever this life has or may bring I will follow you through everything.

Your journey is one never alone. And it will defy all meanings of what use to describe others. This journey I will make with you.

This journey where you and I will follow together. All eternity.

I follow you

You are the intoxicating bridge into the glimpse of where the stars begin, and the earth's sky ends.

You fill my life more than any given scientific mathematical equation.

You, I, share not only voice but passion, fire, lust, life, love.

I hold you as we lay in silence and wrap you into my lips tracing where I can hear your smile grow.

I yearn to feel my touch abide by yours against mine.

One kiss and one kiss another slowly drifting into the moment we awaken further into pleasures we only give each other.

Two bodies into a solidarity merge soul. A feign line star exploding filling every gap into us. We lay held by each other's embrace.

Three rounds maybe more.

Whatever our thirst quench for. Whether in pleasure's touch or holding hands, hearing our laughter in timelessness moments.

When I look into the galaxy that are held into those amorous eyes of yours, I know truth.

The only woman, mine, the one for me, and I, yours.

The only woman for me

ABOUT THE BOOK

This book just continues my words for the endless bound I have for the love of my life. She inspires me not only to write these writings of poetry but inspires me every day to be the very best man I can be. I will always remind her that with me she is not settling but shown why I love her in every way, every day.

Made in the USA
Columbia, SC
30 April 2024